Beyond the Dinosaurs!

Sky Dragons
Sea Monsters
Mega-Mammals
and Other Prehistoric Beasts

by Howard Zimmerman

A BYRON PREISS VISUAL PUBLICATIONS, INC. BOOK

ATHENEUM BOOKS FOR YOUNG READERS
NEW YORK · LONDON · TORONTO · SYDNEY · SINGAPORE

ACKNOWLEDGMENTS
As before, thanks go out to the paleo-art community for the beautiful and visionary art that graces the pages of this book, and to Mike Fredericks at Prehistoric Times for helping to send out the call. Heartfelt thanks also go to Dwight Zimmerman and Kelly Smith for their help in putting the book together. Finally, special thanks to Byron Preiss and Caitlyn Dlouhy for their hard work in making this book possible.

DEDICATION
This book is dedicated to Deane, my wife, best friend, and lifemate, for her support throughout the process. You know, the truth of it is, I couldn't have done this without you.

FRONT ART CREDITS
Page 1: *Quetzalcoatlus* by Jan Sovak
Pages 2 and 3, top: Woolly mammoths by Glen Eisner
Pages 2 and 3, bottom: Blue whale by William Stout
Page 4: Mosaurus by William Stout

Atheneum Books for Young Readers
An imprint of Simon & Schuster Children's Publishing Division
1230 Avenue of the Americas
New York, New York 10020

Interior design by Gilda Hannah
The text of this book is set in Cheltenham.
Printed in Hong Kong

2 4 6 8 10 9 7 5 3 1

Library of Congress Cataloging-in-Publication Data
Zimmerman, Howard.
Beyond the dinosaurs! / Howard Zimmerman.—1st ed.
p.   cm.
ISBN 0-689-84113-2
1. Dinosaurs—Juvenile literature. 2. Animals, Fossil—Juvenile literature.
[1. Prehistoric animals.] I. Title.
QE861.5 .Z56 2001
567.9—dc21   00-056571

FIRST EDITION

CONTENTS

INTRODUCTION

Dinosaurs roamed the Earth for 150 million years. But they are not the only awe-inspiring animals of the distant past. During the time of the dinosaurs fabulous dragons soared the skies and ferocious sea monsters roamed the oceans. And long after they were gone, fantastic giants strode the land.

The dragons of the sky were called pterosaurs (TERR-uh-sawrz), which means "winged lizards." These flying reptiles, great and small, filled the air throughout the Age of Dinosaurs. They were the first creatures to fly, aside from insects.

Fossils of pterosaurs were collected for almost a hundred years before someone figured out what they really were. In 1801, a French scientist named Georges Cuvier (coo-vee-AY) recognized them as ancient reptiles that could fly. He named the fossilized animal he had studied *Pterodactylus*, (terr-uh-DACK-til-us), which means "flight finger." He was referring to the reason these creatures

Pteranodon ingens

could fly. Pterosaurs had a very long fourth finger on each hand. There were flaps of skin connected from the tips of the long fingers to the sides of their bodies. These were the leathery wings of the pterosaurs, which many scientists believe were covered with a kind of downy fur. The fur would have helped keep the animals warm.

Pterosaurs led active lives, like birds. And like birds, they were probably warm-blooded. Some had teeth, but not all did. Some had more teeth than you would believe, like little *Eudimorphodon* (you-dee-MORF-uh-don). Its jaw was only 2 to 4 inches long, but it was filled with 114 sharp, tiny teeth!

*

The dinosaurs stormed the land, and the pterosaurs soared the skies. But they were not alone. In the inland seas and across the worldwide ocean, meat-eating marine reptiles ruled the waves. The larger ones could swallow you whole, and the deadlier ones could follow you onto dry land. These were the sea monsters of the ancient world. Marine reptiles had jaws filled with rows of deadly sharp teeth, and they all ate meat.

These sea monsters lived throughout the entire Age of Dinosaurs, which is called the Mesozoic (mess-uh-ZO-ic) Era. It lasted for 150 million years. The three different time periods of the Mesozoic are called the Triassic (try-ASS-ic), the Jurassic (ju-RASS-ic), and the Cretaceous (kree-TAY-shus).

- The Triassic Period lasted from 245 to 205 million years ago.
- The Jurassic Period lasted from 205 to 140 million years ago.
- The Cretaceous Period lasted from 140 to 65 million years ago.

Some of the flying reptiles, marine reptiles, and dinosaurs may be distantly related. They may each have come from the same line of ancient reptiles. Then, over tens of millions of years, they developed into quite different groups of creatures.

*

Before there were dinosaurs, there were reptiles. And one family of ancient reptiles is quite special. It was their descendents that evolved into the current rulers of the Earth: the mammals. They are called "mammal-like reptiles," or therapsids (ther-AP-sidz). They had odd shapes and strange names, like *Lystrosaurus* (lis-tro-SAW-rus) and *Cynognathus* (sin-og-NAY-thus). They

Plesiosaurus

appeared 50 million years before the dinosaurs and lasted for another 50 million.

After the Age of Dinosaurs, giant mammals and other strange animals dominated the land. Huge, flightless birds chased down and ate small plant-eating mammals. There were giant animals that looked like rhinoceroses and camels, and some that looked like nothing you've ever seen before. There were hulking beasts like the woolly mammoth, an ancient cousin of the modern elephant. Its huge, curved tusks grew to 10 feet or more in length. There were massive plant eaters that looked like a cross between a rhinoceros and a hippopotomus, with names like *Brontotherium* (bron-toe-THER-ee-um) and *Embolotherium* (em-bow-low-THER-ee-um). And there were fierce predators like the saber-toothed tiger—a giant cat with 8-inch-long fangs jutting down from its upper jaws. These were the prehistoric beasts of the Cenozoic (sen-uh-ZO-ic) Era, which has lasted from 65 million years ago to the present. These were the mega-mammals.

We know about all of these strange and fascinating animals from their fossil remains. We know how their bones must have looked and connected when they were alive. While no one knows exactly what color they were, or if they had spots or stripes, many artists work with scientists to bring these animals back to life through their illustrations. Some of the animals here have been painted by more than one artist—each brings his or her own vision to the task, and no two will look the same. But each is as likely to be how the animal looked in life as the other. These are our best guesses.

At the end of the book you can find out how to get more information about these bizarre prehistoric animals and see more of this amazing art. You will see a listing of sites to visit on the World Wide Web. If you can use a computer, or know someone who can do it for you, you can continue to explore these amazing creatures from Earth's astonishing past. But first, let's take a good look at the fabulous sky dragons, sea monsters, and other prehistoric beasts.

American mammoth

Sky Dragons

PTEROSAURS

(TERR-uh-sawrs)

Pterosaurs were the rulers of the skies during the Age of Dinosaurs. They came in many different shapes and sizes. Despite their differences, they were all reptiles. But they were unlike any other group of reptiles that ever lived, because they had the ability to fly. Pterosaurs ate insects, fish, small reptiles, and small mammals. Some may have eaten seeds and berries. Pterosaurs led lives similar to modern birds. But they flew the ancient skies for 70 million years before the first birds appeared.

There were two major types of pterosaurs: long-tailed and short-tailed. The long-tailed pterosaurs came first. Many scientists think the short-tailed pterosaurs evolved from them.

The long-tailed pterosaurs are named the Rhamphorhynchoidea (RAM-for-ink-OID-ee-uh). They had short necks and jaws filled with sharp teeth. The front teeth were longer and more curved than the back ones. This was good for catching fast-moving prey, like flying insects and small fish. Long-tailed pterosaurs soared through the Mesozoic skies from about 170 to 140 million years ago.

The short-tailed pterosaurs are named the Pterodactyloidea (TERR-uh-DACK-till-OID-ee-uh). They had longer necks, and larger bodies in general, than the long-tailed pterosaurs. Many of the short-tailed pterosaurs also had long, bony head crests and long beaks with no teeth. Like all pterosaurs, their bones were lightweight but strong, with air pockets throughout to keep them light. When these reptiles flew, their heads were balanced atop their long necks, like pelicans in flight. They probably lived on fish they scooped up from the seas. The short-tailed pterosaurs ruled the skyways from about 160 to 65 million years ago.

Previous page:
PREONDACTYLUS (pree-on-DACK-til-us). An early long-tailed pterosaur, *Preondactylus* was small, with a wingspan of only 1½ feet. Its wings are short for a pterosaur, and its legs are long. *Preondactylus* means "Preone finger." It was named after the Preone Valley in Italy, where its fossils have been found. It lived from about 230 to 215 million years ago.

Below:
PTERODACTYLUS (terr-uh-DACK-til-lus). *Pterodactylus* was the first pterosaur ("winged lizard") ever discovered. Its name means "flight finger." This flying reptile had a wingspan of about 8 feet. *Pterodactylus* has a whole group of pterosaurs named after it, the Pterodactyloidea (terr-uh-DACK-til-oid-ee-uh). These sky dragons were good flyers. They probably caught and ate flying insects, and also fished for food. Their fossils have been found along what once were ancient seashores. *Pterodactylus* lived in Europe and Africa from about 160 million years ago to 120 million years ago.

Below:
RHAMPHORHYNCHUS (ram-for-INK-us). This long-tailed pterosaur is related to the earliest of the flying reptiles. A whole family is named after it, too: the Rhamphorhynchoidea (ram-for-INK-oid-ee-uh). It was about 3 feet long and had a wingspan of about 5 to 6 feet. At the end of its tail was a rudder-like vane. This helped keep it stable in the air.

Rhamphorhynchus was an agile flyer and ate fish. With its outward-curving, pointy teeth, it didn't have to worry about dropping a meal. *Rhamphorhynchus* means "beak snout." Its fossils have been found in Europe and Africa. It lived from about 170 to 145 million years ago.

Above:
DIMORPHODON (die-MORF-uh-don). This was another early long-tailed pterosaur. Its wingspan was about 4 to 6 feet. It had a large head and long hind legs, with strong claws on its fingers and toes. Scientists think *Dimorphodon* used its claws to climb rocks and cliffs. It may have nested there near lakes or seashores. It ate mostly fish and probably insects, too. *Dimorphodon* means "two-tooth form." The name comes from the fact that it had two kinds of teeth—fangs in front and smaller teeth behind. Its fossils have been found in Europe. It lived from about 215 to 195 million years ago.

Right:
Just because they like fish doesn't mean they'll pass up a meal. Two *Dimorphodons* attack a small reptile. It won't take long before the meal is done and they go hunting again.

Above, top:
SORDES (sore-DEES). A small long-tailed pterosaur, *Sordes* had a wingspan of about 2 to 3 feet. Impressions of its wings have been found in one fossil. They showed that the wings were short and wide. But they also showed something else. Scientists found impressions of hair! *Sordes* had a furry covering over its wings and body. Its name means "hairy evil spirit." Fossils of this pterosaur have been found in North America and Europe. It lived from about 165 to 145 million years ago.

Above, bottom:
BATRACHOGNATHUS (ba-TRACK-og-NAY-thus). This small pterosaur was quite strange. It was a member of the long-tailed family, but it had a short, stubby tail. *Batrachognathus* was a nasty-looking creature with a wide mouth filled with teeth shaped like sharpened pegs. Its name means "flying frog jaw." It was a tiny flying reptile, with a wingspan of only 20 inches, and it ate insects (like frogs do). *Batrachognathus*'s fossils have been found in Europe, where it lived from about 160 to 145 million years ago.

Right:
A *Rhamphorhynchus* swoops down and plucks a fishy meal from a river. The coloring of its downy fur helps it blend in with the plants and trees.

Above, left:
DORYGNATHUS (door-ig-NAY-thus). This pterosaur was built for catching fish on the fly. Its long front teeth curved forward, forming a perfect fish trap. *Dorygnathus* means "spear jaw." It had a wingspan of about 3 feet, and had long hind legs. Its fossils have been found in North America and Europe. *Dorygnathus* lived from about 200 to 185 million years ago.

Above, right:
CAMPLYOGNATHOIDES (cam-plee-og-nuh-THOY-dees). This flying reptile and *Dorygnathus* were similar long-tailed pterosaurs. Both fished for food along the ancient seashores. But *Camplyognathoides* had a shorter head with a curved jaw and smaller teeth. It also had larger eyes and a bigger wingspan, up to 5½ feet. *Camplyognathoides* means "curved jaw." Its fossils have been found in Europe and India, where it lived from about 160 to 145 million years ago.

Below, left:
PETEINOSAURUS (peh-TEEN-uh-SAW-rus). A small, ancient long-tailed pterosaur, *Peteinosaurus* had only a 2-foot wingspan. It had large fangs in the front of its jaws, followed by many smaller, sharp teeth. This was good equipment for catching insects. *Peteinosaurus* means "winged reptile." Its fossils have been found in Europe, where it lived from about 220 to 215 million years ago.

Below, right:
EUDIMORPHODON (yoo-dee-MORF-uh-don). Another ancient long-tail, *Eudimorphodon* is one of the earliest known pterosaurs. It had a wingspan of 3 to 3½ feet. We know what it fed on, as one fossil has been found with the bones of small fish still located in the stomach area. *Eudimorphodon* means "true two-tooth form." It was given this name because even though it was discovered after *Dimorphodon*, it is a more ancient pterosaur with the same two types of teeth. Its fossils have been found in South America and Europe. It lived about 225 to 215 million years ago.

PTERANODON INGENS (terr-an-UH-don IN-genz). There were two kinds of *Pteranodon* (which means "toothless flyer"): *Pteranodon sternbergi* (stern-berg-EE) and *Pteranodon ingens*. *Pteranodon ingens* was one of the largest of the flying reptiles. This short-tailed pterosaur had a lengthy wingspan of 23 to 25 feet. But its skull was even more remarkable. Its lower jaw was over 3 feet long. To balance this, a yard-long bony crest rose from the top of its beak to high over its head. Perhaps more amazing is the fact that this creature only weighed about 35 to 40 pounds. *Pteranodon ingens*'s long, narrow beak had no teeth. It fed on fish it scooped up from the ocean. Its fossils have been found in North America. It lived from about 115 to 70 million years ago.

Below:
A pair of *Pteranodon ingens* get lucky. A marine reptile called a *mosasaur* (MOE-za-sawr) has chased some fish to the surface. The pterosaurs will try to snatch up a meal without becoming one themselves.

Above:
PTERANODON STERNBERGI (terr-an-UH-don stern-BERG-ee). With a 30-foot wingspan, *Pteranodon sternbergi* was the second largest of the flying reptiles. This short-tailed pterosaur had a curved lower jaw that was almost 4 feet long. It had a tall, narrow head crest, which may have helped keep it stable in flight.

    Pteranodon sternbergi's long wings probably enabled it to soar for great distances. It ate fish, which it scooped up with its long toothless beak. It lived at the same time and place as *Pteranodon ingens*: 115 to 70 million years ago in North America.

Right:
TROPEOGNATHUS (TRO-pee-og-NAY-thus). Here was a most unusual-looking pterosaur. This short-tail had two crests, but not on the top of its head. The bony crests came from the front end of its upper and lower jaws. This would have helped to keep the head steady as it flew just above the waves, scooping up fish as it went.

    Tropeognathus had long, curved teeth made for catching and holding on to slippery fish. Its name means "keel jaw," because its jawbones look similar to the keel of a ship. It had a 20-foot wingspan, making it one of the larger pterosaurs. Its fossils have been found in South America. *Tropeognathus* lived from about 120 to 100 million years ago.

Above:
CRIORHYNCHUS (cry-or-INK-us). This large short-tailed pterosaur was a close relative of *Tropeognathus*. It had a wingspan of over 16 feet. *Criorhynchus* had large wings and was a strong flyer. It was probably a fish eater, like *Tropeognathus*. And it, too, had thin bony crests at the top and bottom of its jaws. Scientists think these helped keep the head steady when the pterosaur dipped it in the ocean to fish. *Criorynchus* means "ram-snout." Its fossils have been found in Europe. It lived from about 140 to 90 million years ago.

Below, left:
GALLODACTYLUS (gal-oh-DACK-til-us). A medium-sized ptero-saur, *Gallodactylus* had a wingspan of 4 to 5 feet. It was similar to *Pterodactylus*, but had a short crest at the back of its head. It had long jaws with forward-pointing teeth, but only at the front. Scientists think it ate fish. *Gallodactylus* means "Gallic finger." It was named after France, where its fossils were first found. It lived from about 160 to 145 million years ago.

Below:
GERMANODACTYLUS (ger-man-oh-DACK-til-us). A small short-tail, *Germanodactylus* had a wingspan of about 3 to 4 feet. It had a long, low crest atop its head, running from the middle of its beak to the back of its skull. One of the pair below is using its strong claws to climb a tree, while its mate hangs down, bat-like. Their long, thin jaws held forward-curving teeth—good equipment for catching fish. *Germanodactylus* means "German finger." Its fossils have been found in Europe, where it lived from about 160 to 145 million years ago.

QUETZALCOATLUS (ketz-ul-co-AHT-lus). A flying giant, *Quetzalcoatlus* was the largest and last-known living pterosaur. The wingspan of an adult *Quetzalcoatlus* could reach an astonishing 40 feet or more, making it the size of a small airplane. Fully grown, it probably weighed somewhere around 175 to 210 pounds! This flying reptile had toothless jaws almost 3 feet long, and a short crest at the top of its skull. *Quetzalcoatlus* fossils have been found inland, away from the ancient seas. This leads scientists to believe it was not an ocean fisher. But it might have hunted smaller fish from inland lakes. Some scientists think it was a scavenger, eating animals that were already dead. But no one really knows for sure.

    Quetzalcoatlus fossils were first found in Texas, though the pterosaur was named after a god of ancient Mexican tribes called Quetzalcoatl, who was a giant, feathered serpent. *Quetzalcoatlus* lived in North America about 75 to 65 million years ago.

Right:
A young *Tyrannosaurus rex* makes the mistake of thinking he'll have a meal of flying reptiles. These adult *Quetzalcoatlus* can easily fight off the baby dinosaur.

Left:

DSUNGARIPTERUS (ZUN-gar-IP-ter-us). A medium-sized short-tail, this pterosaur had a wingspan of 9 to 10 feet. Its jaws held short, pointy teeth. Scientists think the powerful jaws may have been used to crack open shellfish like snails and crabs. It might have also eaten fish. *Dsungaripterus* had a narrow, flattened head crest, and was the first to be discovered in China. Its name means "Junggar wing," after the place where its fossils were first found. It lived in Asia and Africa from about 155 to 110 million years ago.

Below:

Quetzalcoatlus was capable of flying vast distances without using much energy. If the wind was at its back, it could soar for miles without ever flapping its enormous wings.

It's feeding time in the Triassic skies. A pair of *Dorygnathus* (top) fight over a squid. Meanwhile, a *Dimorphodon* munches on a meal of fish.

Sea Monsters

THE MARINE REPTILES

There were four major groups of marine reptiles. These were the plesiosaurs and their first cousins the pliosaurs, the mosasaurs, and the ichthyosaurs. Plesiosaurs (PLEZ-ee-uh-sawrs, "almost lizards") were true monsters of the ancient seas. Some of these marine reptiles grew to great lengths, up to 50 feet and more. They swam in all the oceans of the world throughout the Age of Dinosaurs.

The ancestors of the plesiosaurs had once lived on land. But the sea held lots of food, and these reptiles began to spend most of their time in the water. Over millions of years, these animals evolved to become good swimmers. Their arms and hands, legs and feet became huge flippers that moved them through the water. They had stout bodies, short tails, and mouths filled with sharp teeth. Some plesiosaurs had small heads and long necks. Others had shorter necks and larger heads.

Although plesiosaurs lived in water, they were still reptiles. They breathed air, and, like the sea turtles of today, they probably crawled out of the ocean to lay their eggs on the shore.

The short-necked plesiosaurs were better adapted for swimming in deep water, where they could find larger prey. They had big, streamlined bodies, and they were strong swimmers.

The family of marine reptiles called mosasaurs (MOE-za-sawrs) had large heads, short necks, and long tails. Unlike the plesiosaurs, their tails provided more swimming power than their flippers. Mosasaurs had short flippers and swam through the water by moving their long tails from side to side. Their heads were long and their bodies slender. Mosasaurs grew anywhere from 16 to 33 feet long. Their powerful jaws were perfect for cracking open the shells of sea creatures like clams, snails, and ammonites (AM-on-ites). Ammonites are squid-like animals that lived in curled shells. Many ammonite fossils have been found with mosasaur teeth marks on them.

Some mosasaurs were covered in a scaly skin, like modern snakes. Scientists think that mosasaurs are related to the monitor lizard family. They lived about 70 to 65 million years ago. Mosasaur fossils have been found on every continent except Antarctica.

Ichthyosaurs (ICK-thee-uh-SAWRS) were plentiful in the oceans of the Mesozoic Era. They looked like fish, swam like fish, and ate fish. But they were marine reptiles, like the plesiosaurs and the mosasaurs. There were many different kinds of ichthyosaurs, and they came in all sizes. Little *Mixosaurus* was only 3 feet long. But *Shonisaurus* grew to a monstrous length of 50 feet!

The body shape of all ichthyosaurs was streamlined. Some looked like giant tuna, and others looked just like modern dolphins. But they all had body shapes designed for cutting through the water. And they were all excellent swimmers. Unlike other marine reptiles, ichthyosaurs spent their entire lives in the water. They even gave birth to live babies in the water.

Plesiosaurs swam by using their paddle-like flippers. Mosasaurs moved their long bodies and tails from side to side. But ichthyosaurs swam like the sharks of today. They used their powerful tail fins, which were shaped like crescent moons, whipping them quickly from side to side. Many ichthyosaurs could reach speeds of 20 to 25 miles per hour in the water.

The pliosaurs were closely related to the plesiosaurs, and they looked quite similar. But the pliosaurs were a bit larger, more powerful, and probably better swimmers.

Previous page:
The head and long neck of a *Plesiosaurus* rise suddenly from the watery depths as it spots some unsuspecting prey.

A *Tropeognathus* intent on fishing comes dangerously close to the jaws of a plesiosaur.

Above:
MURAENOSAURUS (mur-AY-nuh-saw-rus). The neck of *Muraenosaurus* made up fully half of its 20-foot length. Although its head was small, the jaws were filled with sharp, fish-spearing teeth.

Like all plesiosaurs, its flippers were shaped like the wings of an airplane. Their forward edges were thick and rounded, while the back edges were tapered and thin. This made it easier for the flippers to cut through the water. Plesiosaurs moved their flippers in the same up-and-down flying motion that penguins swim with today.

Muraenosaurus lived about 150 million years ago. Its fossils have been found in Europe.

Right:
MACROPLATA (mac-row-PLA-tuh). This early pliosaur grew to about 15 feet long. It had a crocodile-like skull. The neck was of medium length, about twice that of the head. Unlike the plesiosaurs, the rear flippers were larger in pliosaurs. *Macroplata* ate fish, including the occasional unlucky shark. It lived about 200 million years ago. Its fossils have also been found in Europe.

Left and below:
ELASMOSAURUS (ee-laz-muh-SAW-rus). *Elasmosaurus* had the longest neck of all the plesiosaurs. It grew some 45 to 50 feet long, and 25 feet of that was its neck! It had a small head and huge flippers, the front pair being larger than the rear. It caught and ate fish swimming up near the ocean's surface. It probably wasn't a great swimmer. But it had many, many bones in its long neck, and could curl it around like a snake, catching many fish as it did.

Elasmosaurus means "bony-plate lizard." This refers to the marine reptile's plate-like breastbone and hip bones. It lived from about 80 to 65 million years ago. Its fossils have been found in North America and Asia.

Right and below:
KRONOSAURUS (CROW-nuh-SAW-rus). *Kronosaurus* was the largest of the pliosaurs. It had a short neck, huge head, and powerful jaws filled with needle-sharp teeth. It grew to a monstrous 45 feet in length. Its enormous skull was 9 to 10 feet long. *Kronosaurus* fed in warm, shallow seas that teemed with fish and other ocean creatures.

    Kronosaurus means "Kronos lizard." It was named after Kronos, a mythic giant and the father of the Greek gods. In one story, Kronos eats all of his children! *Kronosaurus* got its name because it was also a giant, and must have had a giant appetite, too. This giant marine reptile lived from about 100 to 65 million years ago. Its fossils have been found in Australia.

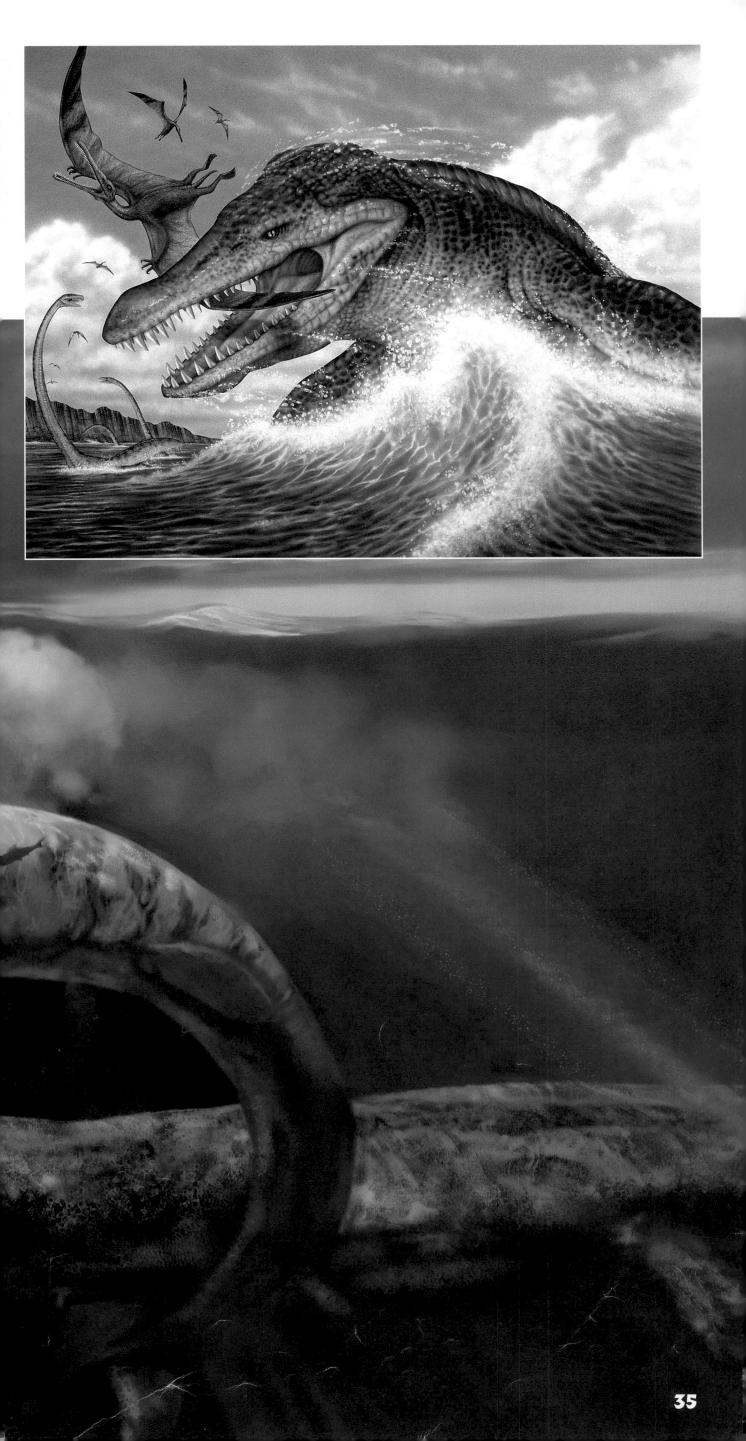

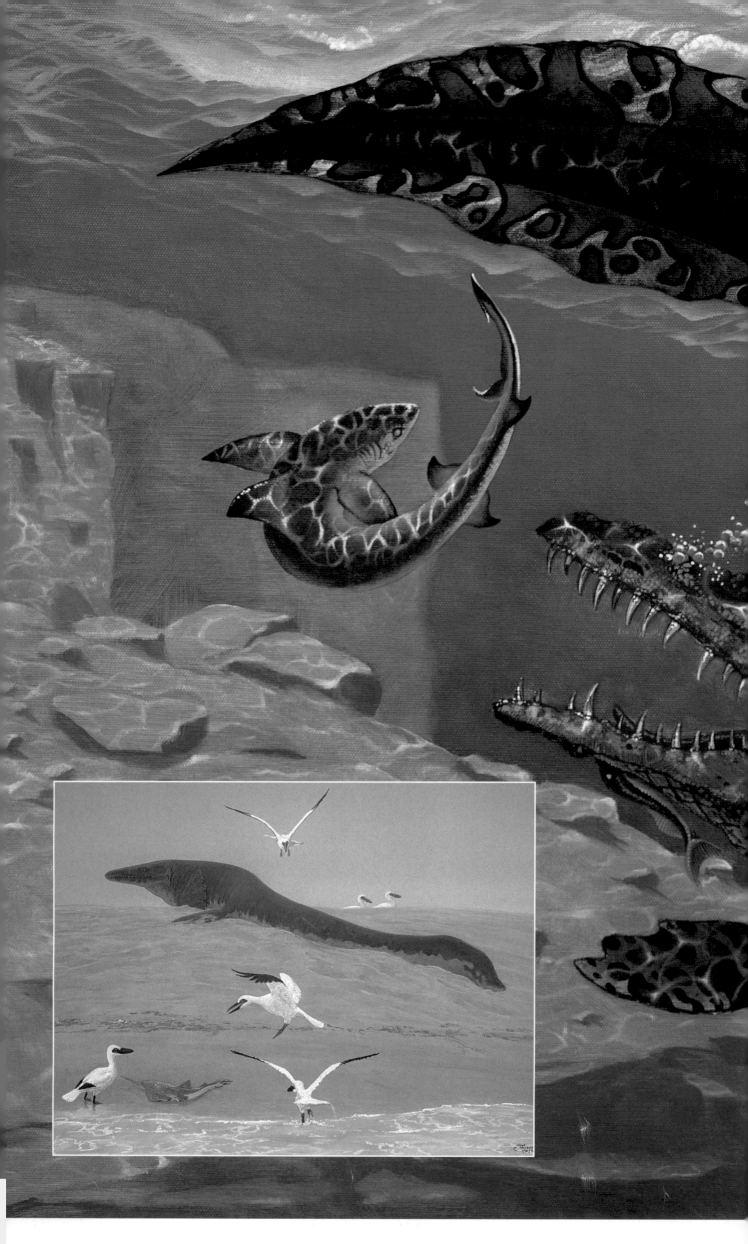

Above:
TYLOSAURUS (TIE-luh-SAW-rus). This mosasaur grew to a length of 23 feet. It had a long skull, about 3 feet long, and a jaw filled with sharp teeth. Its head was covered with bony plates for protection. And its body was covered with lizard-like scales.

The long, deadly jaws of *Tylosaurus* were hinged, like those of a snake. This allowed it to open its mouth very wide and bite off huge chunks of its prey. *Tylosaurus* means

"knobbed lizard." This refers to a round bump on the front of its upper snout. It lived about 70 to 65 million years ago. Its fossils have been found in North America and New Zealand.

Inset:
A female *Mosasaurus* has hauled herself out of the water. She will lay her eggs in the sand.

Right:
OPHTHALMOSAURUS (ahf-THAL-muh-SAW-rus). This medium-sized ichthyosaur was about 12 feet long. It had a streamlined body shaped like a teardrop. The rounded bulk of its front narrowed to the rear of the body, which ended in a large, crescent-moon-shaped tail. *Ophthalmosaurus* had amazingly large eyes, twice the size of other ichthyosaurs. And it had a ring of bony plates around each of them. These helped keep the eyes from collapsing under the pressure of the water—a pressure that grew ever greater when *Ophthalmosaurus* dove after its prey.

Ophthalmosaurus means "eye lizard." Scientists think its keen vision would have allowed it to hunt at night. Like many marine reptiles, its main food was fish and squid. It lived around 150 million years ago. Its fossils have been found in Europe, North America, and South America.

Below:
ICHTHYOSAURUS (ICK-thee-uh-SAW-rus). *Ichthyosaurus* was a medium-sized ichthyosaur. It grew to a length of about 6 to 7 feet long. It was an excellent swimmer, and lived mainly on small fish, shrimp, and squid. As with most of the ichthyosaurs, it had four short flippers, the front pair being longer than the rear. Its nostrils were set far back on its snout, near the eyes. This allowed it to only have to break the water's surface to catch a breath of air.

Ichthyosaurus had an excellent sense of hearing with which to find its prey. But its most potent sense was its sight. It had large, sensitive eyes and could see quite well in the murky depths. Its name means "fish lizard." This refers to the shape of its body, not to its favorite food. *Ichthyosaurus* lived about 200 to 140 million years ago, and its fossils have been found in North America and Europe.

SHONISAURUS (SHOW-nih-SAW-rus). *Shonisaurus* was the largest ichthyosaur that ever lived, reaching an impressive 50 feet in length. One third of its enormous body was taken by the head and neck. Another third was the large, round body, and the final third was its tail.

This monster's jaws were longer than any other ichthyosaur's. Unlike its cousins, *Shonisaurus* had teeth only in the front of its jaws. This arrangement is usually found in animals that eat plants. But these teeth were sharp and curved—*Shonisaurus* was no plant eater! Also different from other ichthyosaurs was the size and shape of its flippers. *Shonisaurus* had long, thin flippers, with the front and rear pairs being the same length—about 5 to 6 feet long. Its name means "Shoshone lizard." It was named after the Shoshone mountains, where its fossils were first found. *Shonisaurus* lived about 200 million years ago. The only complete fossil of this marine reptile was found in North America.

Mega-Mammals
and Other Prehistoric Beasts

Reptiles dominated the prehistoric world for almost 200 million years. There were an amazing variety of them. In the air were the pterosaurs. Riding the waves were the marine reptiles. And on the land was another special group of reptiles, called therapsids. There were many different kinds of therapsids: meat eaters and plant eaters, land animals and those that spent half their time in shallow water. They were large and small, gentle and fierce.

Over the course of 100 million years, therapsids evolved many mammal-like qualities. Perhaps most important, there were therapsids that were warm-blooded and covered in fur. They evolved into the mammals we know today, like dogs and cats, cows and horses, monkeys and people.

Earlier we saw small reptiles that could fly. Here we'll look at a giant bird that couldn't. *Diatryma* (die-uh-TRY-muh) was a member of a bird family called Gruiformes (GROO-ih-forms) which had both strong flyers and flightless birds. Some Gruiformes stood over 10 feet tall. Several were meat eaters that killed and ate reptiles and mammals.

Mammals had been around for much of the Age of Dinosaurs. But they were small, night-hunting animals—no larger than field mice. When the dinosaurs died out, the mammals flourished. They evolved into larger and larger forms of four-legged meat and plant eaters. Some reached giant size, and are referred to as "mega-mammals." Over the course of millions of years, they spread across the globe. They were successful, and ultimately *they* came to dominate the Earth.

Many giant flightless birds and mega-mammals were still living when humans first entered the scene. Humans have no beaks or claws to use as weapons, but we have the ability to make tools. And these tools can be used to fashion the deadliest of weapons. And so the giant carnivores, the previous rulers of the land, became the hunted. Humans helped put an end to some of the flightless birds and mega-mammals with their weapons. Other animals finally died out for different reasons. One was a change of the climate from warm to cold and back to warm again. Another was human destruction of their environments. For example, people began clearing land to plant food. Cutting or burning down bushes, trees, and forests created large fields for planting food like corn and wheat. But it also destroyed the environment of the animals that used to live there.

But all animals must some day pass, no matter how successful they have been. Mammals first appeared soon after the dawn of the Age of Dinosaurs. They've been around for over 220 million years. Many different mammal families have already come and gone. Humans are the dominant animals on Earth now. In time this, too, could change. Then, some strange new creatures may dig up our skeletons and try to figure out what kind of fabulous creatures *we* were!

Previous page:
NORTH AMERICAN MAMMOTH. At 12 feet high, this mega-mammal was larger than the woolly mammoth and just about everything else alive at the time. Its twisting tusks were huge and heavy. The hulking plant eater used them as a modern elephant would, to dig out and knock down plants and trees. They were also used as defensive weapons. This mammoth lived in North America from about 1 million to around 10,000 years ago.

PLACERIAS (pluh-SAIR-ee-us). This big mammal-like reptile lived in the Triassic period, the dawn of the Age of Dinosaurs. It was a forest-dwelling plant eater with strange curved tusks and a beaked jaw. At about 8 feet long, *Placerias* was a large, slow-moving animal. Its name means "broad body." It would have been hunted by packs of smaller, swifter meat-eating dinosaurs.

Placerias was a member of the dicynodont (die-SIN-uh-dont) family. That means "two dog teeth," and refers to the large canine teeth that each dicynodont had. Plant eaters had them as long tusks, and meat eaters had them as long fangs. *Placerias* lived in Africa about 250 million years ago.

Above:

KANNEMEYERIA (can-uh-MIRE-yuh) is attacked by CYNOGNATHUS (sin-og-NAY-thus). A hulking plant eater, *Kannemeyeria* grew to a length of at least 10 feet. Massive bony plates supported its big bulky body. The powerful beak could tear through the toughest of plants. It is named after the scientist who first discovered it, Dr. Kannemeyer. Here one is cornered by a pack of *Cynognathus*—fierce, meat eating dicynodonts. They had sharp fangs and teeth perfect for tearing and cutting flesh. In fact, *Cynognathus* means "dog jaw." Both of these therapsids lived about 140 million years ago in Africa and South America. Fossils of *Kannemeyeria* have also been found in Asia.

Right:

LYSTROSAURUS (lis-truh-SAW-rus). *Lystrosaurus* was another dicynodont. This plant eater also had tusks and a bony beak. *Lystrosaurus* was about 3 to 4 feet long, had a round body, and an oddly flattened face. Its name means "shovel lizard," which refers to the shape of its face and jaw. Scientists believe it may have been a burrowing creature. Here one pauses on high ground to watch the smoke of a distant forest fire. A successful therapsid, *Lystrosaurus* fossils have been found in Africa, Asia, Europe, and even in Antarctica! It lived about 245 million years ago.

Below:
PHORUSRHACUS (for-us-RAKE-us). This flightless bird was a medium-sized Gruiforme. It stood about 5 feet high and had a large head with a sharp, eagle-like beak. It had long, strong legs and was a swift runner. It probably ate anything it could lay a beak or claw on, including reptiles, mammals, birds, and the corpses of dead animals. It lived about 4 to 1 million years ago.

Above:

DINORNIS (dine-OR-nis). *Dinornis* was the largest flightless bird that ever lived. It grew to an astonishing giraffe-like height of 11½ feet! It was part of a family of flightless birds called "moas." Moas evolved in isolation on the island of New Zealand. They grew large and spread all over the island. The oldest moa fossils found were 4 million years old. *Dinornis* had long, heavy legs and a long neck, like all moas. It was a plant eater, and probably lived on fruits, berries, and seeds.

People didn't arrive on New Zealand until around 1,000 years ago. But once there they hunted the flightless birds for food and eventually cleared the forests where the feathered giants lived. The last moas died about 200 years ago.

DIATRYMA (die-uh-TRY-ma). This giant, flightless bird was the terror of its time. Shaped something like a giant eagle, when fully grown it reached a height of 7 to 9 feet. *Diatryma* had thickly muscled legs and three large toes on each foot. Each toe ended in a sharp, thick claw. Its powerful, hooked beak was over a foot long, and was shaped like that of a modern eagle's, but much bigger. *Diatryma*'s head was almost as big as that of a modern horse. It had feathers and wings. But its tiny wings were much too small to enable this huge bird to fly. Its name means "through a hole." This refers to some rather odd holes it had in its foot bones.

The dinosaurs had all died out by the time that *Diatryma* arrived. The mammals alive then were mostly small animals. Many scientists think that *Diatryma* probably hunted them. It was a swift runner, and its claws could easily grab hold of its prey. But not all scientists agree. Some think *Diatryma* was a plant eater. They say that it used its long, sharp beak to cut through the fibers of tough plants.

Diatryma lived on the grasslands of North America and Europe from about 50 million years ago to about 40 million years ago.

A *Diatryma* catches a *Hyracotherium* (hi-rack-uh-THER-ee-um). This little mammal is the earliest known member of the horse family. It is also known as *Eohippus* (ee-oh-HIP-us), or "dawn horse." At only 2 feet long, it was no match for a hungry *Diatryma*.

Right:
PROCOPTODON (pro-COP-tuh-don) and THYLACOLEO (thigh-luh-COLE-ee-oh). *Procoptodon* was a giant kangaroo that grew to over 10 feet long. This plant eater didn't run, but it hopped very quickly. Like modern kangaroos, it could reach speeds of up to 30 miles an hour over short distances. *Procoptodon* means "pounding premolar tooth." This refers to a particular kind of tooth it had. Its premolars were made for mashing plant matter rather than slicing through it.

Like *Procoptodon*, *Thylacoleo* was a marsupial (mar-SOUP-ee-ul). Marsupials are mammals that have pouches, where their babies stay for safety and protection. Unlike the ancient kangaroo, *Thylacoleo* was a lion-like, meat-eating predator. It grew to a length of about 5 to 6 feet. It did not have the fangs of the saber-toothed cats. Instead, its two front top and bottom teeth were long and sharp like chisels. These, and its dagger-like claws, were *Thylacoleo*'s main weapons.

Both of these prehistoric marsupials lived in Australia about 1 million years ago.

Below:
EMBOLOTHERIUM (em-buh-low-THER-ee-um). An immense, rhinoceros-like plant-eating mega-mammal, *Embolotherium* stood 8½ feet high at the shoulder and reached a length of 16 to 20 feet. The horn rising from the top of its snout was connected to another one that covered its face like a mask. Its name, appropriately, means "battering ram beast." It had a small brain, no larger than a man's fist, and lived in Asia from about 50 to 35 million years ago.

Above:
BRONTOTHERIUM (bron-tuh-THER-ee-um). A member of the same family as *Embolotherium*, *Brontotherium* was a bit larger and looked even more rhinoceros-like with its Y-shaped horn. It traveled in herds through forests and woodlands, eating soft plants. It lived from 50–35 million years ago in North America.

Right:
HYAENODONTS (hi-EE-nuh-donts). These early mammals were part of a larger family of flesh-eaters called the creodonts (KREE-uh-donts). They came in many shapes and sizes, from under a foot in length, to yard-long animals (like the pair pictured here), to 6-foot-long ferocious hunters. Hyaenodont means "hyena tooth." Like modern hyenas, hyaenodonts probably scavenged on the bodies of dead animals and also hunted and killed their prey. They lived from about 60 to 30 million years ago. Hyaenodont fossils have been found in North America, Africa, Asia, and Europe.

SMILODON (SMY-luh-don). About 15 million years ago, the Earth became a bit cooler and drier. Vast forests gave way to grassy plains, and a new breed of hunter appeared: the saber-toothed cat. *Smilodon* was one of them. It could blend in with the tall grasses, and quietly stalk its prey. Then, with a leap out in the open, a burst of speed, and a swipe of its powerful paw, it could quickly take down its target.

Modern cats, like lions and tigers, use a "killing bite" to the throat to take down their prey. This kills the prey by either crushing its windpipe or snapping its neck. Saber-toothed cats, on the other hand, used their huge, fang-like teeth to stab their victims to death. The saber-tooth pictured here is *Smilodon*, which means "knife tooth." It was about 5 to 6 feet long and had a short tail, like a modern bobcat. Its powerfully built shoulders and neck muscles enabled it to bite with tremendous force. *Smilodon* lived in North and South America about 5 to 3 million years ago.

Above:
WOOLLY RHINOCEROS. A huge pair of horns distinguishes this plant-eating mega-mammal. The woolly rhinoceros's front horn could grow to an astonishing length of 3 feet or more in an adult male. If it had been solid bone, the rhino may not have been able to lift its head at all! Fortunately, the horn was hollow in the center. Like the woolly mammoth, it also lived in cold climates and had a thick shaggy coat of fur. The woolly rhino grew to a length of 11 to 12 feet. It lived in Europe and Asia from about 1 million to around 15,000 years ago.

Left:
TELEOCERAS (tee-lee-OSS-er-us). This plant-eating mega-mammal was a cross between a rhinoceros and a hippopotamus. *Teleoceras* means "end horn," referring to the horn on the tip of its nose. Its massive, 14-foot-long body was wide and round. Its legs were so short that its belly may have dragged on the ground after a big meal. Like a hippo, *Teleoceras* may have felt more comfortable in the water and probably spent a great deal of time there. The water would have supported its great weight. *Teleoceras* lived 5 to 4 million years ago in North America.

WOOLLY MAMMOTH. Small for its kind, the woolly mammoth stood only about 9 to 10 feet high. It lived in cold climates and had a thick coat of shaggy hair. The dome on the top of its head held a thick layer of fat. This helped keep it warm and may have also provided nutrition when food was scarce. Mammoths were similar to elephants, but lived before them and belonged to their own family. Mammoths were the ruling mega-mammals of their time. Even a saber-tooth would not usually challenge one, but hunger and the scent of young ones might have drawn the cat near. Mammoths lived from about 1 million to around 10,000 years ago. Their fossils have been found in North America, Europe and Asia. Several entire woolly mammoth bodies have been discovered frozen in the Siberian soil.

Mammoths were well adapted for living in the severe cold and harsh conditions of the last Ice Age. They feared no other animal, for few dared to challenge them. A hungry and desperate predator might have tried, but it would not have fared well. And then, humans came along. The size of the mammoths and their long, sharp tusks did not stop people from hunting them, beginning about 20,000 years ago. Here a group of Ice Age hunters try to bring down a baby mammoth using stone-tipped spears. People painted pictures of mammoths on cave walls. Hunting these mega-mammals was dangerous, and may have been an activity that involved the entire tribe.

INDEX

PLACES TO VISIT ON THE WORLD WIDE WEB

Listed below are sites on the World Wide Web that you can visit through your computer, at home, at school, or at the library. Each one is different. Each offers its own special tour through the worlds of the flying and marine reptiles and other fabulous beasts of the distant past.

INTRODUCTION TO THE ICHTHYOSAURIA
http://www.ucmp.berkeley.edu/diapsids/ichthyosauria.html

JUST ABOUT MOSASAURS
http://www.oceansofkansas.com/about-mo.html

THE NATURAL HISTORY MUSEUM, LONDON
http://www.nhm.ac.uk

PALEO RING
http://www.pitt.edu/~mattf/PaleoRing.html

THE PTEROSAUR HOMEPAGE
http://www.home.postnet.com/~azero/Pterosaur_Homepage.htm

THE SMITHSONIAN INSTITUTION
http://www.nmnh.si.edu/departments/paleo.html

UNIVERSITY OF CALIFORNIA MUSEUM OF PALEONTOLOGY
http://www.ucmp.berkeley.edu

ART CREDITS